Conscience Cages

By
Patrick O'Neill

Llumina
PRESS

ISBN: 978-1-62550-489-0

Table of Contents

Preface

This excerpt embodies the nitty-gritties of the nature of the indelible experiences that have inspired, encouraged, and finally badgered me to write this book and all my other books.

✳✳✳

(From "Gardens of Wildernesses: For Phil Kucera."
Conscience Cages. [P.14]):

It's how he
deftly sways me, reluctantly,
to carry my packets
of poems and views
of who I am and what
I perceive to the rich soil
of scheduled,
promoted readings,
to sow, cultivate—
raise crops that will
share their fertility—
grow audiences
to share my work.
It's something painful

I'm determined not to do—
that I'll always find painful.
But it's one of four tasks
I have that grow the only
accomplishments
that I feel good enough about
to keep me believing
it's still worth hanging
around for a while.
From the beginning,
I watch and feel
what he gives of himself
so others—alone, in charge
of themselves—
can grow their discoveries
in exclusive, provocative
gardens of Art.
I can't stop feeling
what he has given me
and how it still serves me:
motivates, energizes—
sends me to scatter seeds
from the kernel of my being
and believe they'll find
fertile ground, take root,
sprout—blossom—bear fruit.

Prologue

Take a look at Colleen, who'll give you an idea of the
kind of characters you'll meet and have to skirmish
with as you wander through the pages of this book:

Colleen banters with her Other Self:

Her Other Self says, "I thought
maybe we could enlist
the lower animals to repair
the ego damage. Now you've
blasted that salvation all to hell."
Colleen says, "We don't need
anyone to service our ego.
Besides the warranty
on our ego expired long ago.
We couldn't pay the price."
"What price?" her Other Self asks.
"The price of individualism—
of suffering the dependency
of animals in zoos,
on farms, on leashes instead
of free ranging. Our ego

has to toughen up
and live with our incompetence,
neglect, and klutzy coordination."
"And," her Other Self adds, "Stupidity."
Colleen nods, reaches over,
strokes Quack Grass,
and pats Big Rock. She says,
"We need to be more like our friends
Quack Grass and Big Rock.
They enjoy the freedom
of not having to battle things
like Conscience Cages."
Her Other Self says, "Yeah,
they do what they do to serve
and enjoy the critters and plants
of their world." Colleen strokes
Quack Grass and says,
"What a beautiful girl!" "GIRL?"
her Other Self shouts.
"How do you know it's a girl?"
"She has," Colleen says,
"that unique female demeanor.
It takes extraordinary independence
to feel comfortable and
to be functional

being the only plant in view
that's growing out of the center
of a huge rock in the middle
of the Montreal River."
She pats the rock. Her Other Self
says, "I suppose you think
Big Rock is a male." Colleen says,
"Of course. It's big and hard
and I'm sitting on it. I'd never sit
on a female—especially a big hard one."
"You have a point," her Other Self says.
Colleen says, "Thanks.
But be careful. Compliments
fire up our Ego and rally the forces
battling to stick us in *that* Cage."
Her Other Self says. "Sorry.
But I was noncommittal.
I didn't say it was a defendable point."
Colleen says, "You have a point."

(From "Big Rock and Quack Grass" [P. 7]).

Conscience Cages

Patsies

Murph, a long-time friend from the west coast, who I haven't been in touch with for over three years, swings into town unexpectedly, calls me, and asks me to speak to his wife about the dependency on institutions she's imposing on their daughter, Luci, a high school junior, and how it's negatively affecting Luci's plans for her future. Murph says his wife won't listen to him but will be a lot more apt to listen to me because I'm neutral, a published writer, and a literature instructor at the college. He tells me his wife reads a lot of poetry and fiction and his daughter Luci has even written some poetry.

A short visit with his wife and Luci tells me institutionalism has captured and caged Luci and is sending her to college to train her to become an institutional tub-thumper. The visit, also tells me I'm not going anywhere with Luci's mother, but Luci sends me vibes that she's listening, thinking, and wondering. She asks me if she can read some of my poetry. I tell her I'll give her a signed copy of one of my books if she'll let me write a poem and dedicate it to her for my next book. She gets excited and asks "Will you really?" Her mother makes a face that that lights a red light about the way things are going. She says, "I don't know if that's a good idea. Maybe . . ." Luci interrupts, "OH, MOM! . . ."—in a tone that seals the deal. Instead of a red light or a green light, her mom flashes me a yellow caution light. I take a chance and consider it green. (I can't write cautiously.) I recklessly write the following poem.

A Poem for Luci

When Pursuit trains
in the training camps
of institutions, he often fights
like hell and destroys Self-Endeavor—
banishing Individualism
and self-esteem. This arrests
healthy development
in our youth. We too often
allow religious, social, political,
and other institutions
determine our children's pursuits
and destinies. Instead

of allowing the children themselves
to experiment and explore—
to discover who they are
and determine their own destinies—
we give them to the institutions
and let the institutions run them
through training programs.
As the children mature,
they become little more
than harnessed, caged patsies
trained to support and promote
the institutions themselves—
believing that *they* deep down
decided their pursuits
and destinies and would have lived
in constant regret and guilt
had they *not* been able to determine
their own destinies—
when the reality is they *didn't.*
And the institutions nod
their approval and gloat.
When it's too late, some will hear
a cry from the distant past
from their Child of Innate Being
asking, "Why? Why did you forsake

me and crawl into the cruel,
self-serving cages of institutions?"
Helpless, they will lament
their innate potential endeavors
that will lie and rot in the past
and never know the challenge
and rewards of fighting
and defeating Evil—never realize
the passionately potent feeling
of the individualistic doubting
and the resulting revelations
leading to self-sacrificing victories
over the forces
of egocentric armies
of Control and Abuse.
Some will answer
their abandoned Innate Children
of the past with a shrug,
some will swear, some will weep.
All will die leaving a legacy
of forced, obscure, self- serving
institutional contributions.
Our children need
to train in the camps
of their own Individualism

and—instead of becoming
institutional patsies—
enlist their innate potential,
energy, and inspiration
to mature their Innate Being.
That will motivate them
to dedicate their lives
to serving on the battlefield
of Good vs. Evil—
fighting the forces
of Egocentric Institutional
Control and Abuse.
Our children need to nourish
and mature their Children
of Innate Being—instead
of nourishing and maturing
institutional patsies.
Then they'll spend their lives
allowing their innate Potential,
Energy, and Inspiration
to lead them to battle
egocentric institutional Control
and Abuse. They'll likely
look back on their lives nodding
and smiling and, as long as they're able,

stay in shape and keep fighting
for what *they're* equipped for
and what their Innate Beings
have driven them decisively
to condemn, confront—
and eliminate or change.
As they continue to look back,
they'll glean the energy
and inspiration to convert or disarm
the patsies of the institutions
of Control and Abuse.

Lawns

Since I was a kid
I've been listening
to manicured lawns
scream in uniform green
that something's wrong.
The pampered plots
lay dormant—foot mats—
little more than showpieces—
squanderers of money, time,
energy. Look at the meadows,
fields, prairies—independent,
courageous plants fighting
for survival alone—
to serve the living
in life and death.
I finally realized
years ago that too many
of us unconsciously
have been using
our mollycoddled lawns
as role models. Instead
of heeding and cultivating
the calls our innate tendencies

to be strong, independent
individuals, we tend
to be pawns, promoting
greed and pretenses.
I tuned in to Nature and caught
the pioneering, independent
spirit of fields, meadows,
and prairies. Now I constantly
fight to escape the cultural
Farm Corporate Conglomerate
that confines us to
cultivated plots, rows:
prunes us; stakes us;
sprays us; genetically alters
us; harvests us—
consumes us
to fuel and maintain
political, religious,
and social machines
that drive the farm
corporations' secret,
ambitious, self-serving
agendas—bearing
proud emblems
that shout: Of the people,
by the people, for the people.

When I attempt to share
this experience and
its philosophical conclusions
with my students
and others who are willing
to listen, I generally get
reactions carrying tones
and implications
that remind me
of my sister's reaction
way back when we were
in high school. I
had just begun seriously
attempting to implement
the philosophy and decided
to try to share it.
When I tried it out on her,
she giggled, then laughed
and said, "You're just desperate
for excuses to get out
of mowing the lawn!"

Big Rock and Quack Grass

Trying to keep her feet dry
and reach Big Rock in the middle
of the Montreal River,
Colleen tight-rope walks
on the small rocks that barely
rise above the swift current
of the River. When she's
on the closest tiny rock to Big Rock,
she leaps; her right foot hits
the sloping surface
of the Big Rock, holds, begins
to slip; her left foot hits
and holds long enough
for her to grab a crag
in Big Rock and pull both feet—
soaking wet—back to solid footing.
She walks up the rock
and sits by the clump
of Quack Grass.
Her Other Self pokes her.
"Nice fucking jump, Klutz Butt."
"Hey, we're here," Colleen says.

"Here"—her Other Self says—
"and not much drier
than the fish that are swimming
around laughing their ass-fins off
at us." Colleen asks, "Since when
do you give a shit
about what the fish think?"
"Since there's not much sense
in wondering what people think,
I thought maybe we could enlist
the lower animals to repair
the ego damage. Now you've
blasted that salvation all to hell."
Colleen says, "We don't need
anyone to service our ego.
Besides the warranty
on our ego expired long ago.
We couldn't pay the price."
"What price?" Her Other Self asks.
"The price of individualism—
of suffering the dependency
of animals in zoos,
on farms, on leashes instead
of free ranging. Our ego
has to toughen up

and live with our incompetence,
neglect, and klutzy coordination."
"And," her Other Self adds, "Stupidity."
Colleen nods, reaches over,
strokes Quack Grass,
and pats Big Rock. She says,
"We need to be more like our friends
Quack Grass and Big Rock.
They enjoy the freedom
of not having to battle things
like Conscience Cages."
Her Other Self says, "Yeah,
they do what they do to serve
and enjoy the critters and plants
of their world." Colleen strokes
Quack Grass and says,
"What a beautiful girl!" "GIRL?"
her Other Self shouts.
"How do you know it's a girl?"
"She has," Colleen says,
"that unique female demeanor.
It takes extraordinary independence
to feel comfortable and
to be functional
being the only plant in view

that's growing out of the center
of a huge rock in the middle
of the Montreal River."
She pats the rock. Her Other Self
says, "I suppose you think
Big Rock is a male." Colleen says,
"Of course. It's big and hard
and I'm sitting on it. I'd never sit
on a female—especially a big hard one."
"You have a point," her Other Self says.
Colleen says, "Thanks.
But be careful. Compliments
fire up our Ego and rally the forces
battling to stick us in *that* Cage."
Her Other Self says. "Sorry.
But I was noncommittal.
I didn't say it was a defendable point.
Colleen says, "You have a point.
After just getting settled on the rock,
Colleen gets into a chatter battle
with a passing otter. With most
of his body out of the water
like, instead of swimming,
he's on stilts, the otter
keeps charging the rock

chatter-scolding her—
for trespassing, she guesses.
Colleen chatter-scolds back
until she tires of the contest
and shuts up. As soon as she
stops, the otter loses interest
and swims away,
looping through the water
like he's playing or showing off—
maybe celebrating his victory
in their chatter contest.
Colleen pats Big Rock,
strokes Quack Grass and visits
with Quack Grass and Big Rock
while she jots down insights
they offer and allows
the right side of her brain
to grasp and hold on to
the inspiration they've radiated.

As the sun sets and darkness
creeps in, she strokes Quack Grass,
rises, plants her feet
on the river bottom, pats
Big Rock, and begins to wade in.

Just then, the swift current
throws Colleen off balance and, slipping
on the slippery river-bottom stones,
she falls. She avoids a drenching
by catching a willow branch hanging
over the river with her left hand
and bracing herself with her right hand
on the river bottom. She pulls
herself to standing and carefully
wades ashore. Her Other Self says,
"Sorry, I hate to do this,
but it's my nature and duty.
So, nice navigating, Klutz Butt!"
"Yeah," Colleen says, "but it's nice
that the fish have me to entertain
them." Her Other Self laughs.
"You're certainly good at that.
You've heard of stand-up comedians.
You're a fall-down comedian."
Colleen says, "Thanks again
for a change. It's the second time today
you complimented me. Fall-down comedy
is spontaneous—a product
of the real me. It clamors sincerity.
It's something the fish can care about

15

and put to good use. You can't fool fish
with artificial feelings—only
with artificial hook-bearing weapons."
Her Other Self says, "Sorry; but my nature
and duty backfired on this one.
The compliment was an accident."
"Sometimes," Colleen says,
"your accidents make more sense
than your intentions." "Thanks.
Ready for another accident?"
her Other Self asks. "Ready," Colleen says.
"That otter," her Other Self says,
"wasn't showing off or playing;
he was laughing his ass off
and applauding the sit-down version
of your fall-down comedy routine."
"Thanks once more," Colleen says
as she makes her way
through the dense riverside brambles.
"Watch your step," her Other Self says.
"I've had enough laughs for one day."
"And," Colleen says, "My mind's
processed enough compliments.
They're swelling my Ego
like a crippled prostate, clogging

those passage ways in the chambers
of my mind that carry ideas, discoveries,
and incentives to invent—and right now
are loaded with the incentives
and contributions of Big Rock
and Quack Grass." Her Other Self says,
"It'd help if you were
more careful too." "Sorry," I say
"but it's not my nature and duty."
At that moment a spruce tree root
that has looped above ground catches
the toe of Colleen's shoe and sends her
to her knees. Her Other Self says,
"Sorry, Klutz Butt,
but it's my nature and duty. . . ."

Back Roads

Custom, Tradition, and Doctrine—
police trained, heavily armed—
band together to curb
unsanctioned affection.
Their relentless sieges drive
Beauty and Truth to the back roads:

Two lovers, faceless nonentities, incognito—
making passionate love in shadows,
in fear, in darkness—exiled
to the crippling obscurity
of censorship.

Birthdays and Deathdays
(*For Grady and Kristy*)

Kristy and Grady:

The contents of this envelope have no connection to celebration but only the expression of feelings that have nothing to do with culture clutches, institutions, or calendars. Use the enclosed to express your sincere, honest, spontaneous feelings for each other.

Buy each other something for your fishing trips, something you need that you've been putting off buying and can put to good use—or you can take each other out for a nutritious* dinner.
Thanks.

*You know my guidelines for a nutritious meal.

The poem:

I wove the material
for the above garment
out of raw hemp I grew
from my experiences

with and observations
of the atrocities
of celebrations.
Like most weaving
a fool attempts,
my weaving never seems
to serve the purpose
I intended it for. I'm
never sure it works.
But I like to feel I've
made an impression.

When they confront
me about the letter,
I tell them: Use it
for what you can do
for each other and others.
Use it to enter the camp
of Action and Service—
not the camp of Inaction
and Rest, where Recuperation
sends you to the state
of stagnant, abusive Idleness—
the death bed of invention
and endeavor—the birth bed

of slough. If you must
celebrate birth, celebrate
the birthdays of your inventive
endeavors, not the birthdays
of your body and mind that
endeavors empower.
Or celebrate the death beds
that your Endeavors make
for your and others' acts
of greed, overindulgence,
addictions, cruelty, etc. They rally;
they seem to get it. *I celebrate.*

My Celebration

To cut calories and come closer to dropping the five pounds I shouldn't be carrying around, I prepare death beds for the extra helpings of bowls of almonds, peanuts, and no-fat yogurt that I reward myself with for my particularly fertile physical and mental endeavors.

I prepare birth beds for a one-mile increase in my early morning six-mile run—and a daily two-hour increase in the time I write, publish books, and to prepare and give readings to finance and promote my Creative Incentive Program for Area Children.

Gardens of Wilderness
(*For Phil Kucera*)

On a tight schedule,
no time to shed
my teaching uniform
(conventional dress-code
costume) and change
into my native skins
(Levis' and sweatshirt),
I hurry into his studio.
Unaccustomed
to my costume,
he pops his eyes; he
doesn't say much.
He grabs his camera,
tells me where to stand—
and, reluctantly, I let him
shoot me a few times—
but I *let* him. That's his style;
It's how he interacts
with people. He banishes
Demand, Control—
generates respect—opening
spacious wildernesses—

forests, meadows,
oceans—for ideas, thoughts
to roam, sail, hike—
to explore, discover,
simplify—or delete
themselves—by themselves.
Those are
the rare spaces
where creativity thrives—
the fertile birthing grounds
of Art. Yeah. It's how he
deftly sways me, reluctantly,
to carry my packets
of poems and views
of who I am and what
I perceive to the rich soil
of scheduled,
promoted readings,
to sow, cultivate—
raise crops that will
share their fertility—
grow audiences
to share my work.
It's something painful
I'm determined not to do—
that I'll always find painful.

But it's one of four tasks
I have that grow the only
accomplishments
that I feel good enough about
to keep me believing
it's still worth hanging
around for a while.
From the beginning,
I watch and feel
what he gives of himself
so others—alone, in charge
of themselves—
can grow their discoveries
in exclusive, provocative
gardens of Art.
I can't stop feeling
what he has given me
and how it still serves me:
motivates, energizes—
sends me to scatter seeds
from the kernel of my being
and believe they'll find
fertile ground, take root,
 sprout—blossom—bear fruit.

Cardboard

After fixing me up with her friend,
my sister, the botanist, warned me.
"She's a history major," she said.
"She hangs out in the past."
I've been with her on my couch
for an hour trying to interest her
in the present. Finally I get her
to kiss me. The kiss takes off
like it's hell bent for *now*.
Then it retreats, flops.
"Cardboard," I say.
"Cardboard?" "Yeah.
The kiss." "What the hell's
a cardboard kiss?"
she asks. "It's one
that starts with fiber,
then folds, collapses. It's
like a cardboard promise,
a cardboard erection,
a cardboard resolution.
Match it against load,
rain, wind and it buckles,

wilts, blows away."
"Metaphorically then,"
she says, "everything's
cardboard. That's not bad;
that's real. There's
a Serbian city called
Cardboard City
where cardboard keeps
hundreds of people alive
in cardboard dwellings.
until the people
buckle, wilt, blow away—
just like mansions, state houses
keep people entertained
until the people
buckle, wilt, blow away.
We're on a cardboard planet
thinking, doing cardboard things—
and you're complaining
about a cardboard kiss?"
"Sorry," I say.
"It was a cardboard complaint."

She puts her arms around me,
says, "This time I'll squeeze

enough fiber into it to record
your cardboard erection
and my cardboard orgasm
for a cardboard posterity."

Late the next morning,
Peg calls her boss and arranges
to take the rest of the day off.
That afternoon my sister calls
and asks, "How'd the date go?"
I say, "I'm not prepared
to give you a full report." "Why?"
She asks. "The date's not over," I say.
NOT OVER?" she yells.
"Don't worry, I say. "We'll have
to bring it to a conclusion soon.
She has to go to work
tomorrow morning." My sister
rants a little more about
how young Peg is (she's
three years younger than me)
and how I'm taking advantage
of her and corrupting her.
I tell her it's the other way around.
I tell her I suggested it was time

for Peg to leave and she refused.
I look at Peg, who's been listening
to some of my side
of the conversation—
nodding and smiling. I hand
her the phone and say,
"Defend me." She says,
"I'll do my best,"
and takes the phone.
I listen to her cardboard words
that ride in a cardboard tone
and decide her cardboard best
is a cardboard defense that'll
earn me a Birdseye-maple,
hardwood lecture
from my sister, the botanist—
the next time she manages
to corner and cage me
long enough to listen.
I'm hoping it's a thin,
flimsy cardboard cage
that collapses as easily
as Peg's initial cardboard -kiss.

Pat O'Neill

Honest

To be honest; to tell the truth; honestly;
honest Injun; honest to God; in all honesty:

Blooper confessions of bold liars. *Honest!*

In The Ring
(*For Vicki*)

Institutions and I
fight regularly.
It gets rough
but not ugly.
We exchange blows
of crushing intent riding
on respect. Loathing
and belittlement stay
out of the ring.
It's like my boxing days.
I'd spar with friends;
we'd beat the hell out
of each other—
then go fishing
or swimming—have
a good time.
As a college instructor,
I fight some of
my toughest bouts.
My fondest memories
are those bouts

when we're in brutal combat,
swinging to lay each other
on the canvas. I can't exist
otherwise within institutions—
and without institutions,
there'd be nothing to fix—
too little to do to feel good about.
Often my punches are
feeble and my timing's off.
I lose fights; but I've won
enough to keep me swinging.
So I write and teach:
throw right crosses, left hooks,
body punches at institutional
restraints/injustices.
Without that, I'd have nothing
to let me imagine that I've KO'd
Commandments that were
determined to beat
the Love, Compassion,
and Tolerance out of virtue.

Ignorance, the Mentor

After years of losing
my grip on endeavors
that I've always regretted
escaped me, I've discovered
that institutional mollycoddling
recruits Fears and Traumas
that enjoy driving us away
from that invisible line
between the past and future.
They send us in both directions—
deep into pleasant distortions
of the past and high
into imagined achievements
of the future. In both locations,
we lose sight of who we are
and where we should allow
our capabilities to take us.
At the same time,
we lose the tools to get there.
Ignorance *is* the mother
and father of wisdom. We need
to quit condemning Ignorance

and embrace her/his wisdom.
Ignorance is a friend—
not an enemy—
whose provocative songs
that we frequently dismiss,
tell stories to challenge
and inspire us to hold tightly
to that invisible/imaginary line
between the past and future
and to trek wildernesses
of what we like to call
the present to explore
and discover instead
of lounging in distant LUXURY—
reminiscing, wishing, and pretending.

Capped?

A grad student observing my lit class
asks me, "Doesn't it frustrate you
when students say they don't understand
a poem or story?" I say, "It irritates me,
not because they don't understand it;
they don't—nor do I or anyone else.
Not understanding ripens opportunities
for exploration that they don't pursue.
They need to delve into the unknown
and communicate the mystery and challenge
that walks point for what they don't understand.
Like anything beautiful, exotic, the unknown
solicits exploration. People expend valuable
time and energy to reach Know—where they
can never go. They crave definitive reinforcement.
In their futile odyssey, they pass by the essence
of what they perceive along the way.
Believing they've arrived where they
can never be shuts out any chance of ever
discovering what they pass." She looks at me,
smiles, says, "I don't understand." "Good," I say,
"neither do I. You trek into your murk;

I'll trek into mine. We'll each decide on vehicles
to send what we discover and deliver it
to wherever it might encourage the launching
of creative expeditions." "What kind of vehicle?"
she asks, "story or poem?" "Naw" I say. "There are
no stories or poems. They're merely names
that distort what the vehicles actually are.
We have unlimited options. Everything
is a vehicle. And we don't understand
any of them. Pick something you feel
uncomfortable about turning loose—
something that burrows deep in your guts,
sends you groping down mysterious trails
not knowing where the next step will take you—
a frightening, enlightening trek." She asks,
"What are you going to use?" "I think I'll go
with a waft of sweat and wintergreen from a gym
in the sixties from what most people called
the Nigger side of Pontiac—where ex-boxers
of questionable qualifications trained young hopefuls
to beat the hell out of each other."
"You?" She wrinkles her brow, thinks awhile,
asks, "You think the frustration of trying
to get there, going nowhere, and the nasty taste
of the pain of failure will trek well?"

Before I can say it, she silences me
with a hand gesture and the tone of voice
you use when you just let words out
of your mouth that don't jive with your thoughts;
she says, "I know, I blindsided that one—
YOU DON'T KNOW." I say, And you don't know
I was going. . . ." She interrupts. "All Right,
all Right," she says, "I don't know that. Let's cap it."
I say, "WE DON'T KNOW." "Capped," she says.
"Maybe" I say; she nods, says, "Maybe not."

Bridging

The recession drove
my brother's bookie
out of Detroit across
the bridge to Canada.
Proposed police department
cutbacks in Detroit spurred
more arrests to justify jobs.
Bookies were easy
but painful pickings.
My brother's bookie
was philosophical.

He said:
       I hold nothing
       against the police.
       We worked well together.
       I hope they're not wrestling
       with their consciences
       about their bookie friends
       and business associates,
       who they arrested or chased
       over the bridge to Canada.
       They did what they had to.

We were in disciplines
on different islands,
but we found ways
to bridge them.
We were cohorts—
but had bumpy times
on those bridges.
A slew of the cops
got the pink slips anyway.
Most of us bookies survived
the recession and the ensuing
police force layoffs.
We still have respectable jobs,
and make decent livings.
We just have to drive
farther and cross
another fucking bridge.
And we'll have to build
more bridges to round up
some more cops
to do business with
and to mother-hen us—
until it's safe
to cross back over the bridge
to our homeland: Detroit.

Brother Bud

You know my brother Bud.
No? Guess most people don't.
Things absorb him;
he fades away
like a squirt of cream
in medium-roast coffee.
He mixes and blends
with his surroundings.
Yeah! Most people
never know he's around,
never pay attention.
It's like he's a shrub
or a pole or a snow bank.
He's got simple ways,
plain features—
nothing highlights him,
or yells for attention.
He blends till he's transparent—
hangs around like a clean pane
of glass. Except sometimes
a faint scent of the earth—
the scent that worms

and mudpuppies wear—wafts
from his wrinkled clothing
and wild hair—puckering
a face here, a face there.
And come to think of it
his limited assortment
of little words
sometimes gather
and power hose
some of the glitter
and murk out
of political poppycock.
Just the other day, a crowd
of those words washed
Mayor Thornton far enough
off-stage to get the Council
to behave like they
had access to thought processes.
Those same words
in different sneakers
started the fiasco that saved
the Senior Center—
redirected that Klan incident
back in September. . . .

Pat O'Neill

Say! You sure you don't know
my brother Bud? Damn funny.
Maybe you don't get around much.

Minnow Motion

My body and eyes quit
communicating.
Body plays tricks on Eyes;
it doesn't reveal
what it's doing.
Eyes play tricks on Body;
they tell Body it's doing
something it isn't.
Mind, oblivious
to their shenanigans,
inadvertently strikes me
with a sickness. Most
know it as motion sickness
that some people experience
in airplanes and boats or ships
on rough waters. But there's
a more serious sickness
that one or more
of my five senses inflict
on *my mind* instead
of my body. It's a virus
that affects thought processes.

It happens most often
when I rely on one or too few
of my senses to engage
my mind in deductive
and inductive thought processes.
Like most people, I tend
to rely too heavily on sight
and sound and come
to conclusions that are
misleading and destructive.
Sight and Sound can block
thorough and insightful analyses
of the evidence we need
to come to sound conclusions.
Otherwise, I'm inclined
to allow the flows, currents,
and surges wash me to something
like one of those wire minnow traps
with the funnel entrance baited
with attractive comforts,
assurances, pacifiers, promises
that lets us in but confronts us
with a tiny nearly
inaccessible opening to exit.
It's a place that washes

away individualistic, creative,
and meaningful actions
that have the potential
to combat these egocentric,
self-serving institutional cages.
I have to do more
to coordinate the troops
of my mind with the troops
of my body motions to find
my balance and to launch
effective strikes against
the institutional troops
to spring me from and keep
me out of their tempting
minnow traps of power,
control, and destruction.

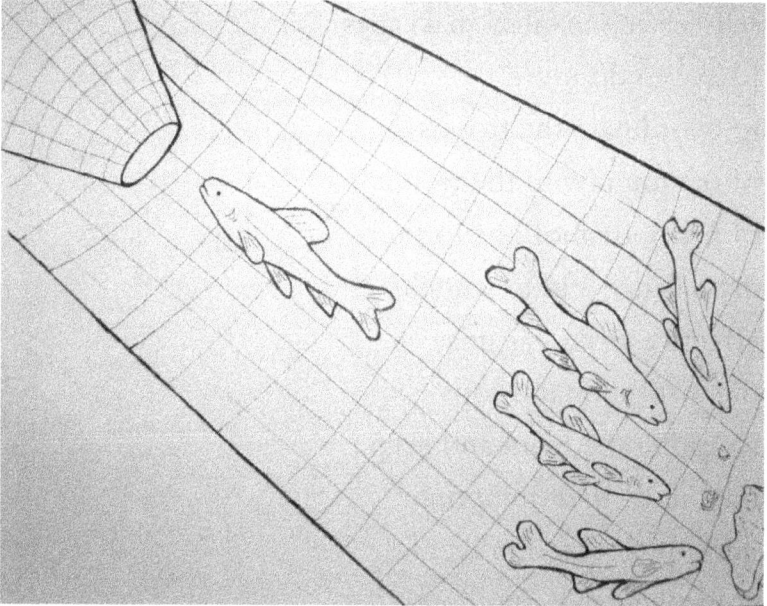

"Minnow Motion"

Toys and Tools

Treat every day
like a brand-new toy,
my niece says
to her uncle Shawn,
who, like me, is allergic
to triteness; he winces
at her expression.
She's justifying her
lackadaisical generally
nonproductive daily activities.
Shawn, recovering
from his allergic reaction
to her trite trope,
says, Toys are for playing.
If you're going to spend
the time scrutinizing
and drawing analogies,
focus on what can lift you
and others to a higher level
of being. What do you suggest?
my niece asks. She looks
at me. I shrug. Shawn says,

you might try brand-new tools.
There's always a better way
to get things done and always
better tools we can invent
to get them done. But beware!
Don't use tools that you
purchase, use, and hang
on hooks in the tool sheds
of your mind.
Keep Inventing your tools.
You can't keep using tools
that other people invent for you.
Use the day as a toolshed
of brand-new tools you invented
in a way only you can use them
to build, discover, and repair.
Laden your work with invention—
not imitation. Shawn and I,
like we rehearsed it, say,
Try it. Wait and see. My niece
looks at me. I nod. Shawn
gives me a thumbs up.
My niece says, You guys
keep taking all the fun out
of the day. She studies the looks

of agreement on our faces
with a frown. Then she flashes
a huge smile and says,
Fun does get in the way
of things. She gets up to leave
and says, Thanks. She opens
the door, turns, and says,
It's been loads of fun, guys,
frowns, smiles,
and flips us a friendly bird.

Don't Know

Preface: I trekked far back in the past and caught and caged the revelation in the following poem. I made my way far enough back to when I knew almost everything—and interrogated myself. Now that I've discovered I don't know anything (and never did), I can assure you that my past and recent experiences and observations that that interacted, mated, and copulated in the beds of the poem's all-encompassing Revelation gave birth to sound, candid conclusions. But, like I say, I don't know.

The Poem:

Knowing—
with the solid backing
of the institutional
backbone of world culture—
beats the fiber out
of feeling and the lifeblood
out of thought. Knowing
blockades passages
to exotic places,

combative elements—
to where we haven't been,
to what we haven't seen.
Knowing kills doubt, crippling
introspective discovery
and invention. Knowing
chases Art underground.
Knowing grows
artificial discovery
and invention
to feed and fertilize
objective, defined goals
that suppress Feeling—
goals that are usually
divisive and destructive.
To even inch toward
a world of unity and peace
that we've only imagined,
we need to give
Feeling more to farm
and harvest—
then let Creativity clear
the way to the rugged,
unexplored wildernesses
of our minds and give

us the courage
and incentive
to pioneer them
and deploy our discoveries
where they'll do the most
to promote and market
 the yields of Feeling's
premier crop: Creativity.

To My Humanities Students

An uncool stranger
who hangs out
in literature
sometimes sucks
distinguishing colors
and shades out
of the narrators' revelations,
spits them in the gutter,
gives the students Grey:
no answers, no boundaries,
no maps, no colors—
just questions and space.

The students snub
the options
and opportunities—
scrap the challenge—
seine in the gutter
for definitive, indelible
black and white.

The Day the Sun Came Up in the West

My Uncle Mac's favorite retort
that he used to underscore
his doubt was, *Yeah!*
And the Sun might come up
in the West tomorrow.
Once, it did come up
in the West for me.
In Kalamazoo, a friend
swung three shifts
at Parchment Paper Mill.
He had the seniority
to work the shift he liked,
but he was hooked
to the diversity,
the alternating routines.
On midnight shift,
he particularly enjoyed
the early-morning
night life atmosphere
in the taverns close
to the mill. When he'd tell

me about it, it seemed farfetched:
women, bands, the works.
He finally got me to meet him
at a tavern on Friday morning
at nine, just as
the midnight shift steamed out
of the mill. We drank our way
through the morning
into the afternoon—then like him—
I headed home for a nap.
When I woke, it was getting light—
the Sun was up. I looked
at the clock; it was 7:10.
I ran to the phone, called
the IGA Market where I worked
the morning shift at seven.
Dick, the manager, answered.
I said, *Dick, sorry—running late;*
I'll be right in. Who's this?
he asked. I told him. He said,
Why the fuck you comin' in?
I said, *It's after seven.*
He laughed, said,
It's Friday evening,
not Saturday morning.

Just to make sure,
I looked out the window
and watched the Sun floating
on the western horizon,
not rising but sinking
like an orange beach ball
with a slow leak. After Dick
finished interrogating me
about how I had deranged
my brain, I went out,
had a couple beers,
and shook my hangover.
The last time I heard
my Uncle Mac use the retort
was at the Memorial Hospital—
after I said to him, *You're tough.*
You'll beat this. Soon, you'll
be up giving it hell.
We'll be wading Cherry Creek,
landing brookies that look
like small northerns.
Then I told him
about the day the Sun
came up in the West.
He laughed, squeezed

my hand, and said, *Goodbye*,
instead of his usual, *See ya, kid*.
That evening he,
like a deflated beach ball,
sank into a darker, deeper
all-encompassing West—
one without an Eastern exit.

The next morning,
I watched the Sun,
obeying a decreed command,
bounce up in the East,
like an orange basketball—
—a solid soldier
with dutiful demeanor
and a cocky smile.

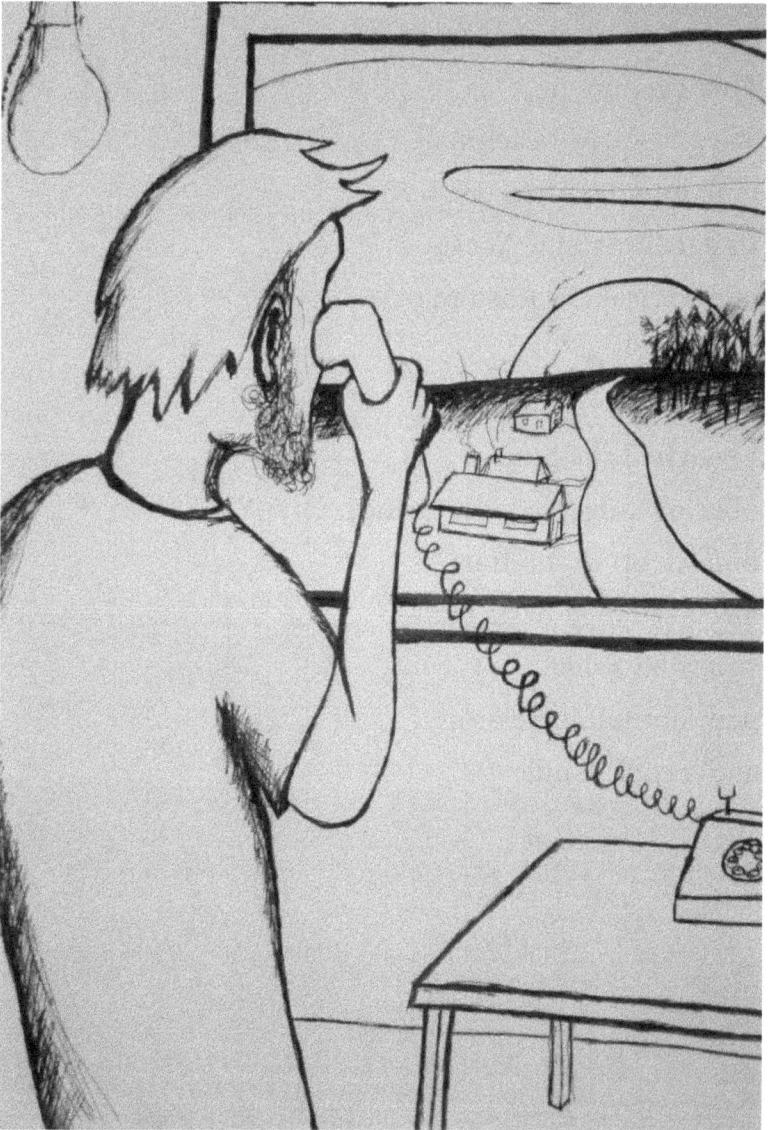

"The Day the Sun Came Up in the West"

Backfire

Civilizations concoct
clusters of climates
that cultivate a contagious,
sterilizing virus
that kills exploratory
and inventive inspiration.
The virus attacks minds
and infects them
with a crippling,
dangerous Conformity,
that condones
only culturally dictated behavior.
Dominating cultural minorities
cultivate and spread
the virus to inflate
their power and control
over oblivious majorities—
who contentedly suffer
the consequences
of the crippling malady—
never discovering
the essence of self—

never realizing the satisfaction
of Discovery and Invention
that plot and battle
for reforms—freedoms.

Meanwhile, the cultures
slowly wither and die.
The ruling minorities discover
too late that the virus they used
to exploit their people has sucked
away at the pulse of what keeps
all cultures vital, vibrant, and alive—
their exotic savior: Creativity.

Fuel

Pain hounds me,
pounds me.
I counter punch
with exploration
and experimentation.
Occasional discoveries
take some steam out
of his punches.
I don't win many rounds
but often propel
myself off the ropes,
throw solid punches—
sometimes pummel him
on the ropes. We haven't yet
hammered each other
to the canvas. Pain's ahead
on points. I won't toss
in the towel. Pain himself
keeps me in the ring—
energized and swinging.
His presence is his nemesis.
I burn him like fuel

A Grand Taste of Profanity

Harry Height, a retired
Great-Lakes boat captain,
swore a lot. It's one reason
neighborhood parents
forbid their kids
to socialize with him.
I—a young, bored, kid—
disobey and discover
a great man who gives
me insights, experiences
that for over fifty years
still cut water
with me. One day,
when I ask him
why he swears,
he says, *Using profanity*
sometimes leaves
a damn fresh, uplifting
taste in my mouth,
like a sharp, November
Lake-Superior wind—
some would say

like Listerine mouth wash
or menthol cough drops.
But like anything
that keeps the ship
afloat and gets us
to where we believe
it's going to make
one hellofa positive
difference, we have
to navigate discreetly.

I never think much
about what he says
until years later
when I realize
there aren't bad or good
words. It is all in how
and why we use them.
I commemorate Harry
from time to time
by launching one
of my several idioms like:

Harry, thanks for the uplifting,
inspirational company. You were

a fuckofa great companion
and teacher on my long voyage
from Dictate and Accept
to Experience and Question—
Real and Right. You gave;
you asked for zilch.
It sends one hellofa sharp
November Lake Superior wind
whistling through my mouth
and whipping
through my mind.

Each time I repeat
a commemorative idiom
for Harry, it doesn't
let me down. The words
leave a vitalizing taste
in my mouth.
The taste gusts
to my psyche—
inspiring, energizing—
kicking the hell out
of regrets,
the doldrums. It's
like a rare, sensitive companion—

maybe the wilderness,
a person, a pet, a river—
an old man. It lifts
the spirit above, beyond
the storms that sink
achievement along
with the satisfaction
that we've navigated
our way through rough waters
with cargo to help rescue
those shipwrecked,
emaciated spirits dying
on islands of despair.

Kinetic

I watch puddles
of inspiration lay, listless
stagnate, and evaporate.
Some of the inspiration
inlets trickle in;
some storm;
some flow;
some stream.
 I have to be alert
to locate, explore, hunt,
and scrutinize them.
They either rush
or sneak in. I force
myself to dive into those
with the most powerful
currents before they
lose their vitality.
It's tempting to ignore
them because once caught
in their currents,
I'm committed.
They compel me

to fight to bust
out of comfortable conformity;
to think, invent, create, give;
to change what lounges
around and doesn't challenge;
to squash what prohibits
or discourages
free thought and expression;
to jumpstart what no longer
charges individual endeavors.
There's nothing more difficult,
time consuming, or painful.
Nor is there anything
as rewarding or refreshing.
Contrary to what most people
who I share this with choose
to think, hunting
and discovering
the raging water,
plunging in, and battling
the current can be
a painful but an invigorating,
adventure of creativity,
invention, and delivery.
Take a plunge.

Pat O'Neill

If nothing else,
it'll be a hellofa good,
rigorous exercise session.

Molt

I watch a wedge
of geese head north
as I paddle a canoe
up the Presque Isle River
with my niece,
an authority on wildlife
and daughter
of my sister, the botanist.
My niece is sitting
in the bow, her paddle idle
on the gunnels.
Front-seat driving, she's
using both hands
and her mouth to point
me to plants she wants
to capture with her camera
for her mother's
plant ecology class.
I ask her why geese
are wedging and heading
north in June. She says,
"Molting season." I ask,

"So what?" She points
at the wedge. "Those,"
she says, "are
the nonbreeders—
geese that are too young
or have lost their mates.
They head north
to small, safer lakes
until they're through molting."
"Why don't the others?" I ask.
She shoots me her mother's
you-stupid-fucker look
and says, "Because the others
have goslings to care for."
"Oh," I say. "Why must they go
to safer lakes to molt?"
She shoots me the same look,
says, "Because while they're
molting they can't fly."
"Oh," I say. I'm not going
to ask her why they all
didn't go to the safer lakes
to begin with. I don't want
to trigger another look;
she flies too high

on flashing her mother's looks.
I'll wait for an opening
to pluck *her* feathers.
She needs periodic molting
to, unlike the young
or unmated geese,
ground her in the big lake—
to help fight the predators,
protect the weak—keep her
from the tempting retreat
to safer lakes. As I paddle
and she shouts and points
the navigation route,
I think a lot about molting.
Before I can avoid it,
a revelation wings in—
like a large goose—
and smacks me.
As I nudge the canoe
against the shore and watch
my niece disembark and begin
snapping shots of a strange-looking
bushy, vine-like plant,
I reluctantly concede
that I, too, need to migrate

to a larger lake, pluck
my comfortable, cozy growth
of debilitating feathers
and grow a new
action-reared crop
that (for the short time I
have left that's streaming
away from me) keeps me air born,
plunging into big-lake challenges—
spurring action, exploration
discovery, invention,
and production:
the life-blood of my Inner Self
who hasn't had enough to do.

Wrong Woos Right

I harvested and processed
the following
from my Uncle Mike, a forester,
as we sat on the stump
of a huge maple he had just felled
that went off course and landed
on his spare chain saw,
 his lunch bucket,
and six pack of Bud Light.
It was way back when I
was a teenager.

I carried the gist of it with me
thirty years before I inadvertently
introduced my uncle to Einstein.
I guess they had a few beers
and teamed up to inspire
and badger me to forge
this vehicle for it:

The Vehicle

When you do something
Wrong, do it wrong right.
Do it with conviction
of following the trail
you forged to the error—
not someone else's trail.
When you clash
with the wrong, fight
to convert it to right—
or raze it so it's inaccessible
to unsuspecting followers
who are apt to embrace
and nourish the wrong—
increasing its potency
in its battle with the Right
that empowered you
to defeat the Wrong.

Einstein pioneered.
His discoveries took him
to a theory that nothing
travels faster than the speed
of light. He was right
and likely wrong. He was

right because all the evidence
he had access to led him
to conclusions that birthed
the theory. Recent discoveries
are singing evidence there's
an element called negoled
that's faster than light.
Einstein's theory opened
new trails—encouraged
exploration and discovery.
Einstein was right
because he named his discovery
Theory—not Fact; all theories
sprout Doubt in fertile,
creative minds.
He doubted he was right.
He planted the theory
to send himself and others
into the unexplored, searching
for something that out races light.
The explorer **Genius** pioneers
the unknown to discover evidence
that contradicts his theories.
His pulse, his vitality is Doubt.
Belief is his deadly predator.

The Avatars

"She's an avatar,"
my niece says. "She runs
around manifesting herself
in different goddess-like shapes
and demeanors—
like slipping
into different bodies
tailored to fit and blend
with the environment
and circumstances."
"Animals do that," I say.
She says, "They do it
to survive. She does it
to infiltrate to attract
and attack—to pilfer
what she doesn't need or have
a right to. She's clever and vicious.
She generally snatches, finagles,
what she's after."
"You and others," I say,
"should point that out to her.
Maybe she's not aware

of her intrusions."
"Not aware! She spends
her time and energy engineering
what you call intrusions.
I call them invasions or attacks.
Her devious intrusions are
what keep her alive.
Her conquests spur her on
to bigger and more challenging
(and profitable) invasions."
"All right, what'd she finagle
or snatch from you?"
How'd you know?" She asks.
I say, "You've written it
all over your face.
All I had to do was decipher it."
"Okay, face reader," she says,
"tell me what it was she snatched
from me." "That," "I say,
was easier to read. You printed
it in large bold caps.
It's **DARREL.**" "Yeah, but it was
only a baby snatch that I
nourished and raised
to become a large adult **dump.**

"You dumped him? I ask."
She nods and says,
"Your guesses were just luck,
right? " "Guesstimates," I say,
"but if you'd brush up
on your cursive scribbling
or just print everything you'd
make it a lot easier on me."
She laughs. "I'll just word process
from now on." "That can't happen,"
I say. "When we deliver messages
from deep inside that ride
on feelings of the moment,
we're confined only to
who we are and how our minds
and bodies decide to deliver them.
That rules out everything exterior
to our being." She nods slowly.
"Technology like computers
would distort it." I nod.
"That's right. It's essential
that feelings and delivery happen
spontaneously and simultaneously."
"This," she says, "is getting
too complicated. We should

get back to what I delivered
and forget how I delivered it."
"I agree." I look at her face intently
and say, "Darrel and the avatar
are still hanging around." She nods.
"How are they treating you?"
She almost smiles. "It's strange,"
she says. "I'll give you a clue.
Your sister, the botanist,
my mom, is celebrating."
I fumble to feign surprise.
She shrugs and smiles
at my feeble attempt and says,
"In a shower of plant
and tree images,
she orated a moving dissertation
plastered with relief, thankfulness,
and I think forgiveness.
I'm surprised she didn't sprinkle
it with tears of joy." I quit pretending
and smile. "Go ahead," she says.
"begin your celebration. Throw
in your 'I-told-you-so pitch."
"Sometimes," I say,
"devious intruders attack

and pilfer what we're
unwisely attempting to hold on to
and inadvertently do us
huge favors." She looks at me, tries
to smile and finally nods and says,
"Darrel was abusive—a self-centered,
selfish avatar himself.
Why did I so desperately
hold on to him?" "Pride," I say.
"You needed to show us
that you had made a decent choice—
that we were wrong. Pride
can take you for reckless rides.
Be careful." She nods, smiles, and says.
"They deserve each other.
I hope they have a long, miserable life
together." I say, "They won't.
When two self-centered avatars
hook up, they realize the misery
each is capable of inflicting
on the other and split before
it happens. They carry with them
the satisfaction of having beaten
others to submission.
They've won." "How sad!"

she says. "It's so unfair. So what
do I do now?" "I'd send her
a thank-you note and him
a congratulations note." She laughs
and says, "I will; I really will.
That should dim their victory glows.
And I should send you and Mom
apology notes." "No. Don't bother,"
I say. "You've already done way more
than you know to make us happy
by dumping Darrel." She says,
"Dumping Darrel;
I like the sound of that." I say,
"Thanks. And while you're
in the dumping mood load up
and dump your other self-centered,
selfish avatar." Who's that?" she asks.
I say, "The reckless, dangerous driver
who started all this. Make sure
if you get in a vehicle
with Pride it's the genuine Pride—
not the avatar." "I promise—
no more gallivanting in the same vehicle
with the avatar Pride. I mean it."
She looks at me hard and with vibe says,

"I *really* mean it!" "I know," I say,
"and I *really* believe it." Still skeptical,
she asks, "Really?" "*Really*!" I say.
"You've printed it in large caps, italics,
and assorted colors on your face."
She laughs, says, "Great" and heads
for the door. I yell after her,
"What's the hurry?" She stops,
turns, and says, "I have to rush
and tell Mom before the thoughts
and feelings that keep running
into each other in both chambers
of my mind inadvertently
distort or erase the powerful message
you read on my face." "Good idea,"
I say. As she turns to leave, I yell again,
"Hey! If you have time on your way,
add a couple illustrations
to your message that will appeal
to your mom's botanical nature."
"Great idea," she yells. Turns to go
and yells back, "I'll toss in a few trees
and plants." She leaves vibrant
and smiling. Before she shuts
the door, I yell, "Give me a call

as soon as your presentation
is over"; and, feeling better
than I have since Darrel
finagled his way into her life,
I sit back and wait for her call.

Epilogue

I'd like you to read my modification of a birthday letter I sent to both of my grandchildren (Deklan, one year old; Miirah, nine years old). I'm hoping as they both become old enough to read and decipher the letter and finally to analyze the content their parents will encourage them to make attempts to understand where I stand and how I feel about what I'm attempting to help them recognize and to fight to keep themselves and others out of the Culture Closets—free to think, explore, and act as individuals.

***

Culture Closets
The Letter:
December 2016
To Deklan/Miirah:

Your being a part of my life for your first years on the planet has helped chase away my painful encounters with hopelessness and self-pity, My gift is a feeble

84

attempt to express my gratitude. I want you to know how much you mean to me and how much you mean to your mother and father and many others. I thank you for what you've done for all of us. And I thank you for what you'll continue to do for those of us who are fortunate enough to be a part of your life for your successive years to come.

An Alert

Don't let institutions lock your independence in Closets of the Culture (like most celebrations) and suffocate your ability to think and act—to discover, invent, and share what only **you** can share instead of contaminated institutional decrees.

***

*"The contents of this envelope have **no connection to celebration** but only the expression of feelings that have nothing to do with culture clutches, institutions, or calendars. Use the enclosed gift to

purchase something that will enable you to express **your** sincere, honest, spontaneous feelings to help enrich your and others' lives."*

*(From the poem "Birthdays and Deathdays" (modified).
[*Conscience Cages* P.13]
Pat
Patrick O'Neill

***